by Umm Assad

Find the Zamzam bottle in every scene!

This book belongs to

_____

Copyright © 2021CE/1442H Umm Assad Publications

All rights reserved. No part of this publication may be reproduced, stored in a retrieval system, or transmitted in any form or by any means, electronic, mechanical, photocopying, recording or otherwise, without the prior permission of the copyright owner.

This book is not intended as a replacement for seeking knowledge. The reader is advised to take full responsibility for safeguarding their knowledge and understanding of Tawheed by regularly referring to authentic sources such as the Qur'an, Sahih ahadith, studying books of Scholars and their trusted students and other than that in the matters relating to his/her religion (Islam).

A catalogue record for this book is available from the British Library.

ISBN-13:   978-0-9957607-3-8
ISBN-10:   099576073X

Author   Umm Assad Bint Jamil Mohammed
Book Design   Umm Assad Bint Jamil Mohammed
Published on   2021CE/1442H

ummassadpublications.com

Bismillahir-Rahmanir-Raheem. Indeed, all praise is for Allah. We praise Him; we seek His help, and we seek His Forgiveness. We seek refuge with Allah from the evil of our own souls and the consequence of our actions. Whomsoever Allah guides, nobody can misguide and whomsoever Allah misguides nobody can guide. I testify that none has the right to be worshipped except Allah alone, He has no partners, and I testify that Muhammad is His slave and Messenger.

DEDICATION

For all the young readers, parents and educators out there, may this book inspire you to keep all your Islamic resources authentic, free from picture-making and unite upon the truth for generations to come!

Umm Assad

In the Arabic language, Sahabah means companions.[2]
When we hear about them, we say,

Radhi-Allahu 'anhum.
May Allah be pleased with them![3]

Their mission was to spread Islam,⁵ so follow their legacy;
To obey Allahﷻ, His Messengerﷺ, then those in authority.⁶

The Prophet Muhammadﷺ said,
"Upon you is to follow my Sunnah and the
Sunnah of the rightly guided Caliphs after me.
Bite on to that with your molar teeth."⁷

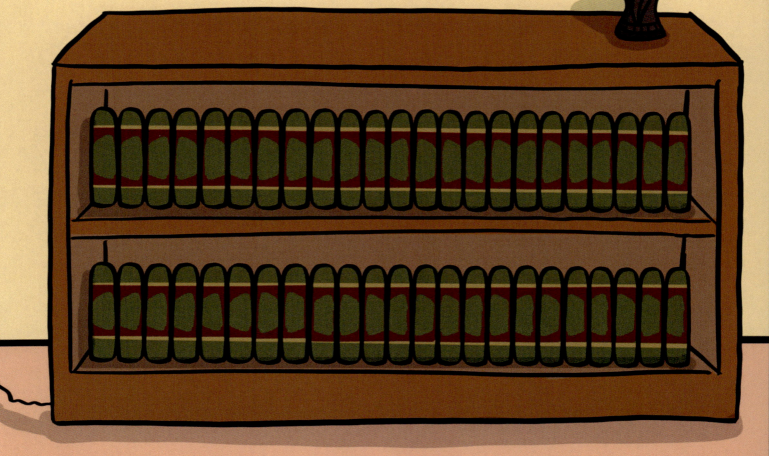

The message of the companions...

Radhi-Allahu 'anhum

Their message was clear, Allah is One; he has no partner or a son, and Muhammad is His servant and Messenger. Say, 'La ilaaha il-Allah, Muhammadar-rasool Allah.' Have firm belief, be steadfast, and you will go to Jannah.[8]

The companions had great love for Allah and His Prophet. They were always ready to defend Islam, and nobody could stop it.

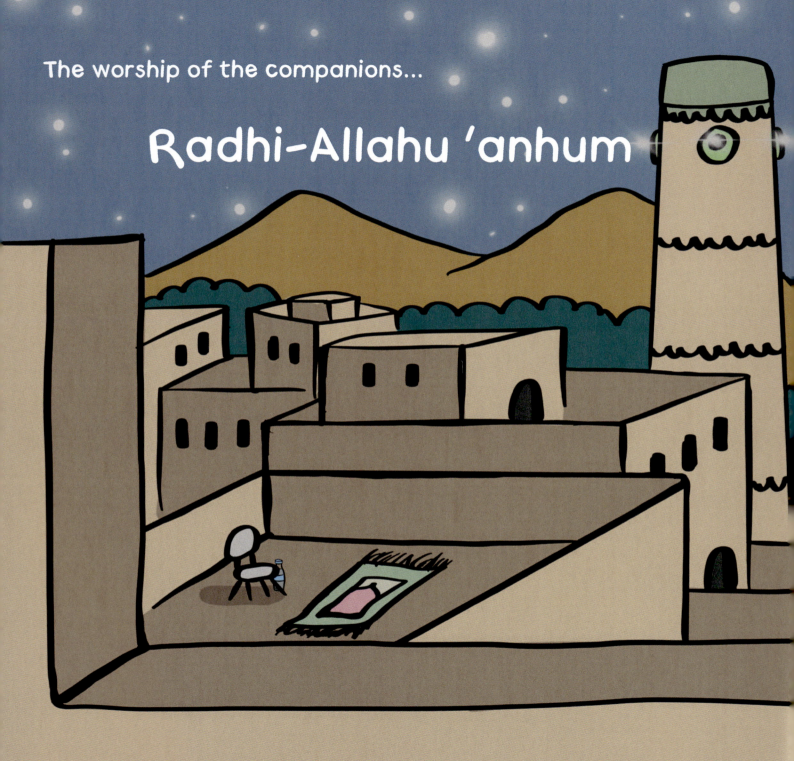

Their worship and deeds were for Allah's ﷻ sake alone.⁹
After the Prophets, they were the best ever known.¹⁰

They prayed like the Prophet ﷺ and fasted in delight.¹¹
They recited and memorised the Quran day and night.¹²
They fed the poor and generously offered charity,¹³
Yet they never neglected themselves or their family.

The manners of the companions...

Radhi-Allahu 'anhum

Their manners and etiquettes were excellent and noble. They treated everyone fairly and were very respectful. They were obedient to their parents, kind to neighbours, Generous to guests, the needy, and helped the believers.[14]

They were not arrogant, rude, lazy, or immodest. They are great role models because they followed the Prophet ﷺ.

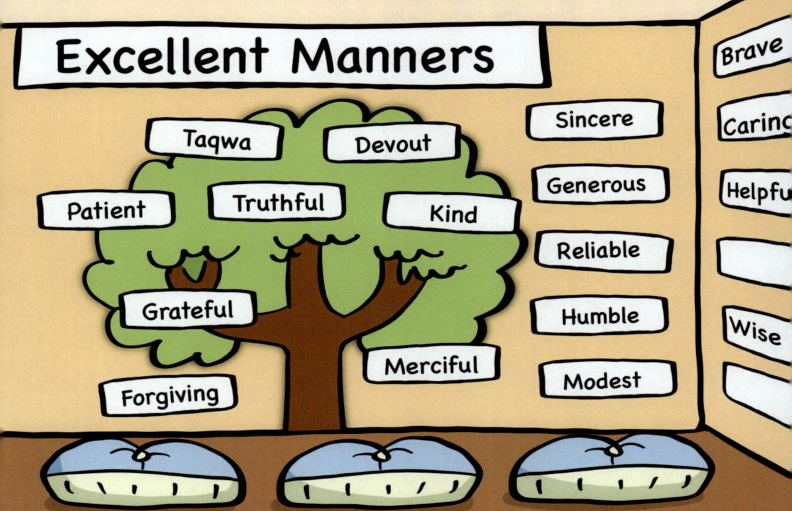

Their status with Allah ﷻ, the Prophet ﷺ and Muslims is great.
Some were superior to others but they were all very great.
Allah ﷻ chose them as witnesses over all of the nations.[15]
The Prophet ﷺ said that the Salaf are the best generation,[16]
Then those who followed them in belief and actions.

Their virtues and rewards are found in both revelations.
Some given high stations, provisions and even big missions.
Allah ﷻ granted them victory, relief and His full protection,
Promised Mercy and Paradise after the oath of allegiance,
And High ranks in beautiful gardens, rivers and mansions.[17]

Their sacrifice included their wealth and their lives.[18]
They dedicated to prove Allah's ﷻ speech is the highest.[19]

They helped the Prophet ﷺ most to aid the call of Islam.
They left their homes behind to migrate to a Muslim land.[20]
They travelled by feet, on donkeys, horses and camels.
Many became martyrs defending the truth in battles.[21]

After they passed away, there was lots of differing.[22]
Bidah spread in the Ummah and many stopped listening.

Their enemies are also the enemies of Allah ﷻ.[23]
They are the people of Kufr, Bidah and Hawaa.[24]

The enemies lie, mock and insult the companions[25]
The believers never mock or insult the companions.
Hating the companions is hypocrisy and disbelief.
Loving and supplicating for the companions is from belief.[26]

The Prophet ﷺ and companions were hated for their unity,
Yet were devout, patient and brave against the enemies.[27]

Their brotherhood was strong, closer than real brothers. They cooperated upon the good,[28] and advised one another. They cared about the knowledge and friends they made, United upon truth, loved and hated for Allah's ﷻ sake.[29]

Now let's have a look at some of their beautiful names...[30]

The best ten companions promised Paradise...³¹

Radhi-Allahu 'anhum

The first four are the rightly guided Caliphs. The Prophet ﷺ called them Al-Khulafaa ar-Raashidoon,³² They are...

Abu Bakr as-Siddiq, The Truthful, First Caliph of Islam
'Umar ibnul-Khattaab, The Second Caliph of Islam
'Uthmaan ibn 'Affaan, The Third Caliph of Islam
'Ali ibn Abu Taalib, The Fourth Caliph of Islam
Az-Zubayr ibnul-'Awwaam, The Disciple
Talhah ibn 'Ubaydillaah, The Living Martyr
'AbdurRahmaan ibn 'Awf, The Wealthiest/Charitable
Sa'd ibn Abu Waqqaas, The Lion in the Deen
Abu 'Ubaydah ibnul-Jarraah, The Nation's Trustworthy
Sa'eed ibn Zayd ibn Amr, Cousin of Umar ibnul-Khattaab

May Allah be pleased with them.

-Those that fought at Badr.³³
Badr is the place where the first battle in Islam took place.

-Those that took the oath of allegiance under the tree of Ar-Ridwaan, at Al-Hudaybiyyah.³⁴
There were about 1500 of them and will not enter the fire.

-The Muhaajiroon.³⁵
Those who migrated from a Mushrik land to a Muslim land.

-The Ansaar.³⁶
'Helpers'; The Muslims of al-Madinah who supported the Muslims who migrated from Makkah.

-Those who became Muslim before the conquest of Makkah
-Those who became Muslim after the conquest of Makkah.

The Prophet's ﷺ daughter Fatimah is also a companion. She will be the first in Paradise from his family to join him And the leader of the Ummah from the believing women.³⁷

May Allah be pleased with them.

They are Umm al-Mu'mineen, Mothers of the believers,[38] and are also promised Paradise. They are...

Khadijah bint Khuwaylid[39]
Sawdah bint Zam'ah[40]
Aishah bint Abu Bakr as-Siddiq[41]
Hafsah bint Umar ibn al-Khattab[42]
Zaynab bint Khuzaymah[43]
Umm-Salamah Hind bint Abu Umayyah[44]
Juwayriyah bint al-Harith[45]
Zaynab bint Jahsh[46]
Umm Habibah Ramlah bint Abu Sufyan[47]
Safiyyah bint Huyay ibn Akhtab[48]
Maymunah bint al-Harith[49]

May Allah be pleased with them.

Every authentic hadith was narrated by a companion. We study the Quran and Sunnah with their understanding. The companions who narrated the most are...

Abu Hurairah who narrated 5374 ahadith
Abdullah ibn Umar ibn Khattab who narrated 2630 ahadith
Anas ibn Maalik who narrated 2286 ahadith
Aisha bint Abu Bakr who narrated 2210 ahadith
Abdullah ibn Abbas who narrated 1660 ahadith
Jaabir ibn Abdullah who narrated 1540 ahadith
Abu Sa'eed al-Khudry who narrated 1170 ahadith

May Allah be pleased with them.

More male companions...

Radhi-Allahu 'anhum

- Abdullah ibn Umar, The Jurist
- Abu Dhar Al-Gifari, Struggle for Equality
- Amr ibn Al-'Aas, The Conqueror of Egypt
- Bilal ibn Rabah, The Mu'adhin (Caller to Prayer)
- Jabir ibn Abdullah, The Example of Sacrifice
- Khabbab ibn Al-Aratt, The Teacher
- Khalid ibn Al-Waleed, The Sword of Allah
- Sa'd ibn Mu'adh, The True Supporter of Islam
- Salman Al-Farisi, In Quest for Truth
- Suhaib Ar-Roomi, The Example of Sacrifice
- Abbas ibn Abdul-Mutalib
- Hamza ibn Abdul-Mutalib
- Abdullah ibn Zubayr
- Mus'ab ibn Umayr
- Ukashah ibn Mihsan
- Abdullah Ibn Mas'ud
- Muadh ibn Jabal
- Zaid ibn Thabit
- Julaybeeb

May Allah be pleased with them.

More female companions…

Radhi-Allahu 'anhum

- Fatimah, The Daughter of the Prophet
- Umm Kulthum, The Daughter of the Prophet
- Ruqayyah, The Daughter of the Prophet
- Zaynab, The Daughter of the Prophet
- Asma bint Abu Bakr as-Siddiq
- Asma bint Umays
- Asma bint Yazid ibn as-Sakn
- Umm Kulthum bint 'Uqbah
- Zaynab bint Abu Salamah, Stepdaughter of the Prophet
- Umm al-Fadl, Mother of six noble companions
- Umm 'Imarah Nusaybah bint Ka'b ibn Amr ibn 'Awf
- Umm Sulaym Rumaysa
- Barirah, The Freed Slave of Aishah
- Sumayah bint Khayaat – The First Martyr
- Umm Haram bint Milhan, The Martyr
- Umm Atiyyah Nasibah bint al-Harith
- Ar-Rubayyi bint Mu'awwidh
- Fatimah bint Asad ibn Hashim
- Fatimah bint Qays

May Allah be pleased with them.

The final companions...

Radhi-Allahu 'anhum

Umm Khalid bint Khalid, the last female companion to leave this world, migrated from Abyssinia. She was a little girl.

The Prophet ﷺ gifted her a garment, prayed she lives long, And no women lived as long as she did after he was gone.[51]

Abu Tufayl 'Aamir ibn Waathilah, the final companion to pass away. He saw the Prophet ﷺ at the farewell Hajj and was just a boy that day.

He was about 8 years old when the Prophet passed away. He was about 100 years old when he finally passed away.[52]

Finally...

We study the Sunnah of the Prophet ﷺ and companions
To understand their status, creed, and follow their actions.

There are thousands of companions[53] and we love them all.
We ask Allah ﷻ to grant them His mercy and a great reward
To let us enter Paradise where we can be with them all.[54]

When we hear about them, we say...

Radhi-Allahu 'anhum.
May Allah be pleased with them all!

Glossary

Allah: The Name of The One True God
'Aqeedah: Belief
Abi: My Father
Sahabah/Sahabi: Companion of the Prophet; someone that met the Prophet, believed in him and died upon Islam.
Radhi-Allahu 'Anhum/'Anhu/'Anha: May Allah be pleased with them/him/her
Islam: To worship Allah alone and not join partners with Him
Muslim: The one who submits to Allah alone
Salaf: Predecessors; the early Muslims of the first three generations; the companions, the Successors and their successors
Ummah: The Muslim nation
Tawheed: Allah is the only Lord of creation. He alone is the provider and sustainer. Allah has Names and Attributes that none of the creation share and Allah is to be singled out for worship, alone. Tawheed is maintaining the Oneness of Allah in all the categories mentioned above. Islam makes a clear distinction between the Creator and the created
Shirk: Associating partners with Allah; compromising any aspect of *Tawheed*
Mushrik: Polytheists, pagans, and disbelievers in the Oneness of Allah and His Messenger
Bidah: Innovation in the religion of Islam
Kufr: Disbelief in the religion of Islam
Hawaa: Desires
La ilaaha il-Allah: There is no deity worth of worthy in truth except for Allah alone
Muhammadar-rasool Allah: Muhammad is the messenger of Allah
Jannah: Paradise
Dua: Supplication
Qur'an: Speech of Allah, Revelation from Allah
Shahadah: To bear witness
Salah: Prayer
Zakah: Obligatory charity for those who are able
Sawm: Fasting
Hajj: Pilgrimage to Makkah
Taqwa: Acting in obedience to Allah, hoping for His Mercy, and leaving acts of disobedience, out of fear of Him
Al-Khulafaa ar-Raashidoon: Rightly guided caliphs
Badr: The place where the first battle in Islam took place
Ansar: 'Helpers'; The Muslims of al-Madinah who supported the Muslims who migrated from Makkah
Muhaajiroon: Immigrants; those who migrated to the land of Islam from the land of Shirk
Hijrah: To migrate to the land of Islam from the land of Shirk
Umm al-Mu'mineen: Mother of the believers
Sunnah/Hadith: Teachings, sayings, approval of the Prophet regarding the Religion of Islam

Glyphs

 - May the peace and blessings of Allah be upon him

 - May He be glorified and exalted (referring to Allah)

 - May Allah be pleased with them all.

 - May Allah be pleased with him.

- May Allah be pleased with her.

Endnotes

1. Quran: Surah 12, Ayah 3.
2. Quran: Surah 9, Ayah 40.
3. Quran: Surah 9, Ayah 100.
4. Al-Isaaba by Ibn Hajr.
5. Quran: Surah 9, Ayah 71. Quran: Surah 2, Ayah 143.
6. Quran: Surah 4, Ayah 59.
7. Hadith: English Translation of Sunan Abu Dawud, Volume 5, The Book of Sunnah, Hadith 4607.
8. Quran: Surah 112. Quran: Surah 3, Ayah 18. Quran: Surah 33, Ayah 40. Quran: Surah 41, Ayah 30.
9. Quran: Surah 39, Ayah 11.
10. Quran: Surah 4, Ayah 69. Quran: Surah 3, Ayah 110. Hadith: Sahih Al-Bukhari Translation Arabic-English, Volume 5, The Virtues of The Companions of The Prophet, Hadith [3650].
11. Quran: Surah 48, Ayah 29, Quran: Surah 33, Ayah 35, Quran: Surah 22, Ayah 77. Sahih Al-Bukhari Translation Arabic-English, Volume 1, The Book of Adhan, Hadith [631]. Sahih Al-Bukhari Translation Arabic-English, Volume 1, The Book of Adhan, Hadith [757]
12. Quran: Surah 35, Ayah 31.
13. Quran: Surah 4, Ayah 162. Hadith: English Translation of Musnad Imam Ahmad Bin Hanbal, Volume 1, Musnad Uthman bin Affan, Hadith 420, Hadith 511. **Hadith:** Sahih Al-Bukhari Translation Arabic-English, Volume 5, The Virtues of The Companions of The Prophet, Hadith [3673].

14. Quran: Surah 16, Ayah 128, Quran: Surah 4, Ayah 135, Quran: Surah 2, Ayah 143, Quran: Surah 3, Ayah 200. Hadith: Sahih Al-Bukhari Translation Arabic-English, Volume 8, The Book of Al-Adab (Good Manners), Hadith [6018].
15. Quran: Surah 22, Ayah 78. Quran: Surah 2, Ayah 143. ran: Surah 4, Ayah 135. Quran: Surah 4, Ayah 59. QuHadith: Sahih Al-Bukhari Translation Arabic-English, Volume 5, The Virtues of The Companions of The Prophet, Hadith [3650].
16. Hadith: Sahih Al-Bukhari Translation Arabic-English, Volume 8, The Book of Asking Permission, Hadith [6285, 6286]. Hadith: English Translation of Sunan Ibn Majah, Volume 2, Chapters Regarding Funerals, Hadith 1621.
17. Quran: Surah 110. Quran: Surah 16, Ayah 128. Quran: Surah 2, Ayah 143. Quran: Surah 9, Ayah 72, Quran: Surah 5, Ayah 9, Quran: Surah 47, Ayah 15, Quran: Surah 32, Ayah 17. Quran: Surah 48, Ayah 18, Hadith: Sahih Al-Bukhari Translation Arabic-English, Volume 4, The Book of Jihad, Hadith [2960]
18. Quran: Surah 61, Ayah 11. Quran: Surah 22, Ayah 78. Quran: Surah 6, Ayah 162.
19. Hadith: English Translation of Sahih Muslim, Volume 2, The Book of Jumu'ah, Hadith [2005] 43 - (867)
20. Quran: Surah 9, Ayah 100, Quran: Surah 8, Ayah 74, Quran: Surah 59, Ayah 8.
21. Quran: Surah 57, Ayah 19, Quran: Surah 4, Ayah 69, Quran: Surah 33, Ayah 23
22. Hadith: English Translation of Sunan Abu Dawud, Volume 5, The Book of Sunnah, Hadith 4607. Hadith: English Translation of Sunan Abu Dawud, Volume 5, The Book of Sunnah, Hadith 4596. Hadith: English Translation of Sunan Ibn Majah, Volume 5, Chapters On Tribulations, Hadith 3993.
23. Quran: Surah 60, Ayah 1, Quran: Surah 4, Ayah 45, Quran: Surah 4, Ayah 101, Quran: Surah 41, Ayah 28, Quran: Surah 6, Ayah 112
24. Quran: Surah 98, Ayah 6. Quran: Surah 4, Ayah 48. Quran: Surah 3, Ayah 85. Quran: Surah 28, Ayah 50. Quran: Surah 2, Ayah 120, Ayah 145. Quran: Surah 45, Ayah 23. Quran: Surah 4, Ayah 145. Hadith: English Translation of Sunan Abu Dawud, Volume 5, The Book of The Sunnah, Hadith 4607.
25. Quran: Surah 2, Ayah 146, Quran: Surah 2, Ayah 14, Quran: Surah 2, Ayah 212, Quran: Surah 4, Ayah 46, Quran: Surah 4, Ayah 140,
26. Quran: Surah 59, Ayah 10, Hadith: Sahih Al-Bukhari Translation Arabic-English, Volume 5, The Merits of Al-Ansar, Hadith [3784]. Sahih Al-Bukhari Translation Arabic-English, Volume 1, The Book of Belief, Hadith [17].
27. Quran: Surah 47, Ayah 35. Quran: Surah 110. Quran: Surah 48, Ayah 29. Quran: Surah 3, Ayah 200.
28. Quran: Surah 5, Ayah 2.
29. Quran: Surah 4, Ayah 69. Quran: Surah 48, Ayah 29. Quran: Surah 5, Ayah 2. Quran: Surah 103. Hadith: Sahih Al-Bukhari Translation Arabic-English, Volume 5, The Virtues of The Companions of the Prophet, Hadith [3688]. Hadith: English Translation of Sahih Muslim, Volume 6, The Book of Al-Birr, Hadith [6548] 37 - (2566). Hadith: English Translation of Jami' At-Tirmidhi, Volume 4, Chapters on Zuhd, Hadith 2390.
30. Al-Isaaba by Ibn Hajr.
31. Hadith: English Translation of Jami' At-Tirmidhi, Volume 6, Chapters on Al-Manaqib, Hadith 3747, 3748.
32. Hadith: English Translation of Sunan Abu Dawud, Volume 5, The Book of Sunnah, Hadith 4607
33. Quran: Surah 3, Ayah 13, Ayah 123, Quran: Surah 8, Ayah 41, Ayah 44. Hadith: Sahih Al-Bukhari Translation Arabic-English, Volume 6, The Book of Commentary, Hadith [4595]. Hadith: Sahih Al-Bukhari Translation Arabic-English, Volume 4, The Book of Jihad, Hadith [3007].
34. Quran: Surah 48, Ayah 18, Hadith: Sahih Al-Bukhari Translation Arabic-English, Volume 4, The Book of Jihad, Hadith [2960]
35. Quran: Surah 2, Ayah 13, Quran: Surah 9, Ayah 100, Ayah 117
36. Quran: Surah 2, Ayah 13, Quran: Surah 9, Ayah 100, Ayah 117
37. Hadith: Sahih Al-Bukhari Translation Arabic-English, Volume 8, The Book of Asking Permission, Hadith [6285, 6286]. Hadith: English Translation of Sunan Ibn Majah, Volume 2, Chapters Regarding Funerals, Hadith 1621.
38. Quran: Surah 33, Ayah 6.
39. Hadith: Sahih Al-Bukhari Translation Arabic-English, Volume 9, The Book of Tauhid, Hadith [7484]. Hadith: English Translation of Sahih Muslim, Volume 6, Virtues of The Companions, Hadith [6276] 73 - (2434)
40. Sunan An-Anasa'i compiled by Imam Hafiz Abu Abdur Rahman Ahmad bin Shu"aib bin 'Ali An-Nasa'i, Translated by Nasiruddin al-Khattab [Volume 3, The Book of Zakah, Chapter 59, The Virtue of Charity Hadith 2542, Page 368]
41. Hadith: Sahih Al-Bukhari Translation Arabic-English, Volume 5, The Virtues of The Companions of The Prophet, Hadith [3662]. Hadith: English Translation of Sahih Muslim, Volume 6, Virtues of The Companions, Hadith [6177] 8 - (2384)
42. Sunan An-Anasa'i compiled by Imam Hafiz Abu Abdur Rahman Ahmad bin Shu"aib bin 'Ali An-Nasa'i, Translated by Nasiruddin al-Khattab [Volume 4, The Book of Marriage, Chapter 24, A Man Offering His Daughter in Marriage to Someone Whom He Likes, Hadith 3250, Page 112, 113]
43. Al-Isaaba by Ibn Hajr 13/426.
44. Sunan An-Anasa'i compiled by Imam Hafiz Abu Abdur Rahman Ahmad bin Shu"aib bin 'Ali An-Nasa'i, Translated by Nasiruddin al-Khattab [Volume 4, The Book of Marriage, Chapter 44, Stepdaughter Who Is In One's Care Is Forbidden For Marriage, Hadith 3286, Page 131, 132]
45. Hadith: English Translation of Sunan Abu Dawud, Volume 4, The Book of Manumission of Slaves, Hadith 3931 (Hasan by Al-Albani)
46. Quran: Surah 33, Ayah 37. Hadith: Sahih Al-Bukhari Translation Arabic-English, Volume 9, The Book of Tauhid, Hadith [7420], [7421]. Hadith: Sahih Al-Bukhari Translation Arabic-English, Volume 2, The Book of Zakat, Hadith [1420].
47. Hadith: English Translation of Sunan Abu Dawud, Volume 2, The Book of Marriage, Hadith 2107
48. Hadith: English Translation of Sunan Abu Dawud, Volume 3, The Book of Kharaj, Fai' And Imarah (Leadership), Hadith 2998
49. Sunan An-Anasa'i compiled by Imam Hafiz Abu Abdur Rahman Ahmad bin Shu"aib bin 'Ali An-Nasa'i, Translated by Nasiruddin al-Khattab [Volume 3, The Mawaqit, Chapter 90, The Concession Allowing A Muhrim To Get Married, Hadith 2840, Page 522,523]
50. Al-Isaaba by Ibn Hajr
51. Hadith: Sahih Al-Bukhari Translation Arabic-English, Volume 7, The Book of Dress, Hadith [5845]
52. Hadith: English Translation of Sahih Muslim, Volume 6, Virtues of The Companions, Hadith [6481] 218 - (2538)
53. Hadith: Sahih Al-Bukhari Translation Arabic-English, Volume 8, The Book of Ar-Riqaq, Hadith [6542, 6543].
54. Quran: Surah 4, Ayah 69, Quran: Surah 5, Ayah 84. Hadith: English Translation of Jami' At-Tirmidhi, Volume 4, The Description of Paradise, Hadith 2546.

Note: For more references, please refer to authentic sources such as: Al-Quran and Al-Kutub As-Sab'ah (The Seven Books): Sahih Al-Bukhari, Sahih Muslim, Sunan Abu Dawud, Sunan At-Tirmidhi, Sunan An-Nasa'I, Sunan ibn Majah, Musnad Ahmad.

ABOUT THE AUTHOR:

Umm Assad has had a great love for helping others since early childhood. She has cared for the elderly, adults and preschool children. Umm Assad also enjoys seeking knowledge and writing to express her lessons in life. Over the years, this passion has seen her create unique books, children's educational resources and even poetry of which some she now enjoys sharing.

Some of Umm Assad's best-selling titles are the 'Allah is One' Series and 'The Prophet Muhammad'.

Other books by Umm Assad:

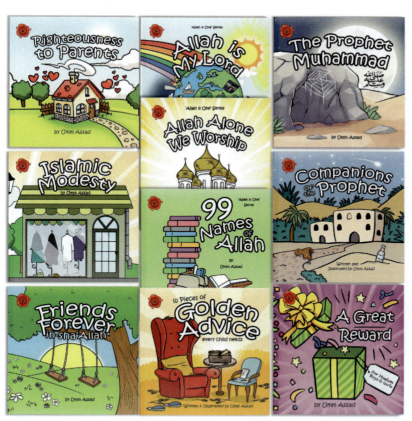

You can contact Umm Assad where you can also download your free 'Islamic Activity Pack' to use alongside her books:

Websites:
ummassadpublications.com,
ummassadhomeschool.com

Twitter: ummassadpubs
Instagram: ummassad.pubs
Facebook: ummassadpubs
Youtube: ummassadpublications

ummassadpublications.com
'Take Pride in Authenticity'